The Parables of Jesus

Scripture text from
The Contemporary English Version

Master
Books

CHAPTER 1

The Sower

Vincent van Gogh (1853-1890), "Crows in a Cornfield," 1890

The colors in the painting are vibrant and strong. The brush strokes are bold. The artist wants to capture the scene and share it. What catches your eye? What catches your imagination?

© Artephot / A. Held, Van Gogh Museum, Amsterdam (Netherlands)

Jesus' Teaching

There were many farmers at the time of Jesus. They worked the ground and sowed the grain by hand, scattering it widely. The seeds fell everywhere. Sometimes the soil was not very good. Quite a lot of seeds were lost and produced no fruit.*

Jesus used the image of a farmer to teach about the Kingdom of God. It's just like seeds of corn sown by hand in a field. Some are lost, but when harvest time comes, each seed is capable of producing thirty, sixty, or even a hundred new seeds. The power of the Kingdom is greater than anyone can imagine.

"The Sower," Stained-glass window in the Church of St Joseph at Haguenau (France)

Harvest Time

Those who traveled with Jesus heard this story and were entertained and interested. But they did not always understand its deeper meaning.**

Forty Years Later

"Saint Mark," Orthodox Church of St Gabriel, Nazareth (Israel)

Forty years later when Mark wrote his Gospel, he used the parable of the farmer. When he writes it down and explains it, he is thinking about those who will hear it. They are no longer the crowds in Judea, as in Jesus' day, but the people living in Rome.*** These people are not Jews but Christians. They no longer hear Jesus' actual voice, but instead they hear the Good News told by those who followed Jesus. Mark calls this "the word" or "the message."

* Producing fruit
Under the best conditions you might expect twenty new grains for every one you sow, but the normal number was ten for every one sown.

** Deeper meaning
Jesus often speaks in parables. They are very simple stories to understand, but they have a hidden and deeper meaning.

*** People living in Rome
Mark, who was a friend of the apostle Paul, probably wrote his Gospel in Rome shortly after A.D. 60.

3

Four Types of Soil

Mark 4.3-9, 13-20

Now listen! A farmer went out to scatter seed in a field. While the farmer was scattering the seed, some of it fell along the road and was eaten by birds. Other seeds fell on thin, rocky ground and quickly started growing because the soil wasn't very deep. But when the sun came up, the plants were scorched and dried up, because they did not have enough roots. Some other seeds fell where thornbushes grew up and choked out the plants. So they did not produce any grain. But a few seeds did fall on good ground where the plants grew and produced thirty or sixty or even a hundred times as much as was scattered.

Then Jesus said, "If you have ears, pay attention."

Jesus told them:

If you don't understand this story, you won't understand any others. What the farmer is spreading is really the message about the kingdom. The seeds that fell along the road are the people who hear the message. But Satan soon comes and snatches it away from them. The seeds that fell on rocky ground are the people who gladly hear the message and accept it right away. But they don't have any roots, and they don't last very long. As soon as life goes hard or the message gets them in trouble, they give up.

The seeds that fell among the thornbushes are also people who hear the message. But they start worrying about the needs of this life. They are fooled by the desire to get rich and to have all kinds of other things. So the message gets choked out, and they never produce anything. The seeds that fell on good ground are the people who hear and welcome the message. They produce thirty or sixty or even a hundred times as much as was planted.

The Sower

This story is usually called The Parable of the Farmer or Sower. Really, it would be better to call it The Parable of the Soils.

The Message

After hearing Jesus' explanation, the listeners can reflect on the question of how much or how little each of them welcomes the Good News.

Persecution

The Christians in Rome, for whom Mark was writing his Gospel, were persecuted in A.D. 64 by Emperor Nero. They were wrongly accused of setting fire to the city.

What Type of Soil Will the Good Seed Fall On?

It Doesn't Sink in

Some people hear everything that is said to them. They are not deaf, but what you say to them is just more noise in a noisy world. These people hear, but they do not listen. Whatever is said to them is like water rolling off a duck's back. We call them "impermeable." It means that we can't get through to them. Nothing sinks in.

Soon Forgotten

Some people hear what is said to them. They become really interested, but they don't remember what they've just been told! They are preoccupied with so many other things. Their minds are clogged up with their own worries, many of which are unnecessary. What they hear seems to make no difference. They soon forget!

Doing Something

Some people take in what they are told. They take it to heart. It's as if they open the door of their house and say, "Come in! There's nothing to distract us. Make yourself at home. What do you want to say to us?" They really listen to what is said to them and treasure it in their mind and hearts. They let it change them and say, "What can we do?"

Jesus the Word

Jesus Christ is the Word. You can hear his message about God's love in all he said and did. You can recognize the hope he brought to the world and take his Gospel to heart. Listening to the Word means taking it to heart as you hear the Gospel message read or read it for yourselves. You can also hear Jesus speak in everything people do to sow seeds that help us to love God and our neighbor.

Fruits

We are the soil
where the word is sown,
the gospel word
Christ will make our own.

If we hear his word,
make a home for his truth,
the gospel he speaks
will bear much fruit.

We can do great things
with his word in our hearts:
    be truthful
    live reconciled
    forgive those who hurt us
    make peace
    be generous with what is ours
    when we pray, say "Our Father"
    spread the riches of love
    make a home for the poor
    help people denied a land of their
    own
    use our strength for those pushed
    aside
    work with energy to bring
    happiness.

These are the fruits
that show we have heard
and taken to heart
Christ's gospel word.

CHAPTER 2

The Good Samaritan

The two figures make one image. The flowing lines express strength and helplessness. What do you see? What do you like? How does the artist catch your attention?

Camille Claus,
The Good Samaritan

© Camille Claus, Church of Gunstett (France)

Jesus Answers with a Parable

The desert between Jerusalem and Jericho

The "smart" people, the teachers of the Law of Moses and the chief priests didn't like Jesus. They were out to get him because he disturbed them with what he said.* So they tried to embarrass him and trap him with difficult questions. Jesus didn't let them get away with it. He knew their tricks.

One day someone asked him, "What must I do to have eternal life?" "You know what to do," replied Jesus. "You know the Law: Love the Lord God and love your neighbor." "Yes," said the man, "but who is my neighbor?" Jesus' answer was a story about a man who was attacked by robbers in the countryside.** He was left for dead. Three men passed by. Which of them would be a good neighbor and help the wounded man? Not the one you would expect.

Saint Luke, Church of St Stephen, Jerusalem

Luke's Account

"What matters is what we do for our neighbor."

Luke*** is the only gospel writer to tell the story of the man attacked by robbers. When he tells it, he's not speaking to the teachers of the Law, as Jesus had been, but to Christians in a different country. Some had been Jews and others had worshiped different gods. To the Jews, such people were foreigners.

Luke wants them to understand three things:

1. Jesus continued teaching what was in the Law of Moses: "You must love God and your neighbor!"
2. Jesus took this teaching further. From now on your neighbor is not just the person next door or the people who live in your country, but every human being… even those who are despised.
3. The Samaritan (the foreigner) is closer to God than the priest or the Levite. What matters is not where you come from. It's what you do for your neighbor.

* He disturbed them
This is because the way Jesus taught was different from other teachers of the Law. "He taught with authority and not like the teachers of the Law of Moses." (Mark 1.22).

** The countryside
This refers to the dry and empty countryside between Jerusalem and Jericho. The distance is about eighteen miles, and it is a lonely road where it is easy for robbers to lie in wait for travelers.

*** Luke
Luke probably wrote his Gospel around A.D. 80. This was about fifty years after Jesus' public ministry.

B i b l e

Who Is My Neighbor?

Luke 10.25-37

An expert in the Law of Moses stood up and asked Jesus a question to see what he would say. "Teacher," he asked, "what must I do to have eternal life?"

Jesus answered, "What is written in the Scriptures? How do you understand them?"

The man replied, "The Scriptures say, 'Love the Lord your God with all your heart, soul, strength, and mind.' They also say, 'Love your neighbors as much as you love yourself.'"

Jesus said, "You have given the right answer. If you do this, you will have eternal life."

But the man wanted to show that he knew what he was talking about. So he asked Jesus, "Who are my neighbors?"

Jesus replied:

As a man was going down from Jerusalem to Jericho, robbers attacked him and grabbed everything he had. They beat him up and ran off, leaving him half dead.

A priest happened to be going down the same road. But when he saw the man, he walked by on the other side. Later a temple helper came to the same place. But when he saw the man who had been beaten up, he also went by on the other side.

A man from Samaria then came traveling along that road. When he saw the man, he felt sorry for him and went over to him. He treated his wounds with olive oil and wine and bandaged them. Then he put him on his own donkey and took him to an inn, where he took care of him. The next morning he gave the innkeeper two silver coins and said, "Please take care of the man. If you spend more than this on him, I will pay you when I return."

Then Jesus asked, "Which one of these three people was a real neighbor to the man who was beaten up by robbers?"

The teacher answered, "The one who showed pity."

Jesus said, "Go and do the same!"

A Priest
and a Levite

These are representatives of the official Jewish religion. They are often seen in the Temple. They ought to be very faithful to the Law and help people in distress.

A Samaritan

Jews thought of Samaritans as enemies and looked down on them. No one expected anything good from a Samaritan.

Do the Same

You – a teacher of the Law who asked this question about who your neighbor is – learn a lesson from this Samaritan you look down on so much!

11

Becoming a Neighbor

Your Neighbors

It's all in the word: neighbors! Your neighbors are those persons near to you, even if you've become so used to them that you hardly notice them any more! Neighbors are part of daily life. They cross your path every day. You meet them throughout life. Whether near or far away, your neighbors are those who need your help, who need you to be there, who need your support and your love!

Passing by

Why do we sometimes feel distant from our neighbors? What makes us pass them by without bothering about them? It's probably because we're afraid of getting too involved if we notice them and ask what they need from us. It's usually because we're worried that their ways and needs will disturb our lives. Often it's easier to pretend that we haven't noticed them.

Getting Close

There can be only one thing to do when we come across someone in distress: try to help that person and offer some relief. This means letting people see that we're on their side so that they will not be afraid or feel alone in their trouble. Getting close to your neighbors means helping them find the strength and freedom to be the persons they are created to be.

Modern-day Samaritans

You can find a Good Samaritan today whenever a person responds to a cry for help. Samaritans are people who don't limit the time they offer or worry about how much help they will give. They don't pick and choose whom to help. They help anyone, without distinction, because they understand that we're all people in need of help. They have only one concern: not to take too long in responding to someone who needs help.

Over to You

You can choose to be
a Good Samaritan!

You can give time
when friends at school
need help to catch up.

You can give words
for someone new
and people left out.

You can make room
for others in your life
so it's not just about "me."

You can listen, not mock,
when people have ideas
different from your own.

You can show respect
for differences of color
or ethnic background.

You can take time
to find words and ways
to comfort people in need.

And you can make time
to pray for the courage
and joy
it takes to be
a Good Samaritan.

The Pharisee and the Tax Collector

Pierre Subleyras
(1699-1749),
The Meal at Simon's House

Jesus is at dinner at the house of Simon the Pharisee. The woman kneeling at his feet has washed his feet with her tears and dried them with her hair. Other guests are shocked. They whisper to one another, "Doesn't he know she's a sinner?" You can read the story for yourself in Luke 7.36-50. The picture is crowded with details. How does the artist use them to tell the story?

© Photo RMN - Hervé Lewandowski, Louvre Museum, Paris (France)

The "Good" and the "Bad"

Statue of a Roman Dignitary.
Port of Caesarea (Israel)

In Jesus' day it was common to label people. They put the "good people" on one side and the "bad people" on the other, those who obeyed the Law of Moses on one side and sinners on the other. The Pharisees thought of themselves as being completely righteous and just. They believed they were entirely faithful to the Law. The tax collectors were regarded as sinners.

The Pharisees were dedicated to obeying the Law of Moses in every detail. They called themselves the "people apart." They were a group set apart from the High Priests and from the ordinary people whom they looked down on and considered "impure."

There were only about six thousand of them, but they had a great influence on the country, on business, on the ordinary people, and even on the priests. They were the ones who explained how the Law was to be applied in day-to-day life.*

The tax collectors were despised because they worked for the Romans. It was their job to collect the taxes and to charge taxes for the Customs Service – a tax on imports. The amounts were fixed by the authorities, but the tax collectors often asked for more and then kept the extra for themselves. They were rich but were detested by the people.

Jesus welcomed both Pharisees and tax collectors.** In everything he did he showed that sinners who repent and turn back to God are closer to God than those who believe they are righteous and without sin because they obey the Law.

Dead Sea Scroll, Qumran (Israel)

What Counts

"What counts is to recognize humbly who we are."

Much later, when Luke wrote down this parable, he was not talking to Pharisees and tax collectors. He was talking to Christians who prayed and thought themselves better than others. He tells them that it's no use showing off, even if you are doing something you think is good. What counts with God is to recognize humbly who we are.

* Pharisees
Flavius Josephus, a first century writer said, "The Pharisees are considered to be more pious than the other Jews and more detailed in their explanations of the Law."

** Tax collectors
Jesus went to eat at various people's homes, with Simon the Pharisee (Luke 7.36-50) and with the tax collector called Zacchaeus (Luke 19.1-10).

15

Two Men

Luke 18.9-14

Jesus told a story to some people who thought they were better than others and who looked down on everyone else:

Two men went into the temple to pray. One was a Pharisee and the other a tax collector.

The Pharisee stood over by himself and prayed, "God, I thank you that I am not greedy, dishonest, and unfaithful in marriage like other people. And I am really glad that I am not like that tax collector over there. I go without eating for two days a week, and I give you one tenth of all I earn."

The tax collector stood off at a distance and did not think he was good enough even to look up toward heaven. He was so sorry for what he had done that he pounded his chest and prayed, "God, have pity on me! I am such a sinner."

Then Jesus said, "When the two men went home, it was the tax collector and not the Pharisee who was pleasing to God. If you put yourself above others, you will be put down. But if you humble yourself, you will be honored."

Their Own Goodness

This refers to the Pharisees who considered themselves to be good because they observed the Law in every detail. They trusted in their own goodness instead of in God's.

Like Everyone Else

The Pharisee twice compares himself to poor people who are not as "good" as he is since they do not observe the Law as carefully. The tax collector, on the other hand, doesn't compare himself to anyone. He speaks of himself as a helpless sinner who must depend solely on God's gracious love.

Two Days a Week

The Pharisee is very boastful. The Law demanded that people fast only one day a year, and that the ten percent tax (tithe) was not required on everything.

Good or Bad?

Sinners

Everyone is bothered by a tendency to sin. Apart from Jesus Christ, everyone at times lets sin into his or her life. All of us behave at times in a way that has nothing to do with loving God and our neighbor. Being a sinner means living in a way that is far from God and our neighbor. But in God's eyes, a sinner is not kept a prisoner of sin forever.

Categories

People love to make lists of who's good and who's bad. They put people into categories and label them: "She's good!" "He's a sinner!" When they do this, they end up judging people without pity and rejecting them: "Those people aren't worth bothering about! Keep clear of them! You'll only get dragged down to their level!" Blaming people and putting them into categories means that we put ourselves at the very top of the list!

Superior

Some people believe that they are the best and are superior to others. They think they're obeying God's commandments so perfectly that no one can complain about them and, therefore, they are pure. According to them, they steer clear of sin. They are convinced that everything they say is true and that they have the right to the best places in the sight of God. They don't need other people!

Humble

Some people are aware of their weakness. They try their best to keep God's commandments and follow the Gospel of Jesus. They don't always manage this: it's hard, and they recognize it! They think of themselves as human like everyone else, with both good qualities and bad faults. They don't get puffed up with pride. They ask forgiveness. They count on God's love and others.

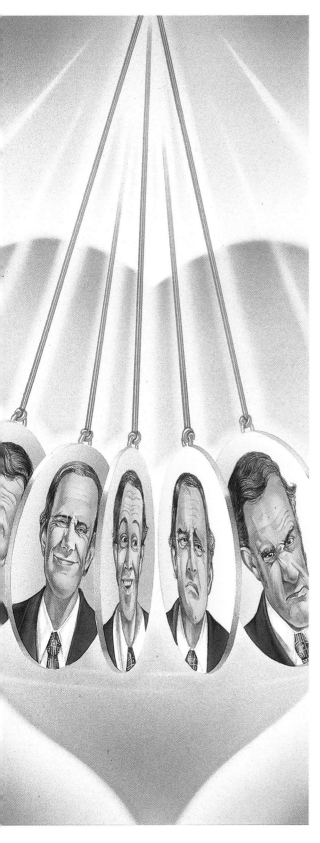

You Know Me, Lord

I come before you, Lord,
without any fear
and full of trust!

You know perfectly well
the secrets of my heart
and why I do what I do!
Other people just
see what's on the surface!
But you, Lord,
see inside me
and you love me.

I am a sinner;
you know it, Lord,
I set out for the truth
but sometimes end up in lies;
I help people in need
and comfort those in trouble,
but sometimes I do it just to look good.

I worship you and I pray, Lord,
but sometimes I end up
forgetting your message.
I'm full of courage
to journey on the path
of your Gospel of light,
but sometimes I lose heart
and want to give up completely.

That's what I'm like, Lord.
And that's how
you love me!

CHAPTER 4

The Prodigal Son

The artist creates a picture that is like a symbol. The son is a robot-like figure without a face. The figure of the father is the bright light in the painting as he reaches out to welcome his son. What do you think the artist's message is?

Giorgio de Chirico (1888-1978), The Prodigal Son, 1922

© Lauros-Giraudon / ADAGP, Paris 1999, Modern Art Gallery, Milan (Italy)

No Difference

"No difference"

Jesus didn't reject people. He welcomed everyone — those who were considered "good" as well as the others.* His acceptance of such "outsiders" angered the scribes and the Pharisees. It was a scandal to welcome people who didn't keep the Law. To help people understand his way of acting Jesus told stories. One of his stories was about a lost sheep. The shepherd leaves his other sheep to look for his one lost sheep, and when he finds it, he is very happy. Another of Jesus' stories is about a woman who loses some money. She looks for it everywhere. When she finds it, she rejoices with her friends. Still another is about a man who watches his son walk away from his home and family. When the boy comes back, the father is overcome with joy and throws a party. Each one of these stories, or parables, teaches the same thing: when you find something that you had lost, you're happy. It's true for us, and it's true for God.

"Young Shepherd" (Syria)

God's Love

"Parable of the Prodigal Son," stained-glass window from the church at Wasperwiller (France)

Luke did not meet Jesus in person, so he never heard Jesus telling the parables himself. The first Christians kept a record of Jesus' teachings,** and it was from them that Luke found out about the story of the son who left and later returned home and was welcomed by his father. In his Gospel, Luke was not telling these parables to a crowd as Jesus did. Luke had traveled a lot and had thought about all the rich and poor people he met along the way, the Jews and the foreigners, the "good" people and the "sinners." He wanted to show them all what God's love is like for a sinner who comes back. Jesus had said that it's like a loving, elderly father who goes running out to meet his rebellious son. Older men don't usually run because it's not thought of as dignified. But the happy father did it anyway to celebrate his son's return.

* As well as the others
The "others" included tax collectors whom the people hated, a Samaritan woman who was looked down on by people, and a Roman soldier who was a pagan.

** Jesus' teachings
In the villages where Jesus had traveled and taught, people kept on telling the stories that we call parables. The first Christians gradually came to understand them more deeply, and they sometimes adapted them to fit new situations.

The Father's Love

Luke 15.11-24

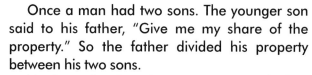

Once a man had two sons. The younger son said to his father, "Give me my share of the property." So the father divided his property between his two sons.

Not long after that, the younger son packed up everything he owned and left for a foreign country, where he wasted all his money in wild living. He had spent everything, when a bad famine spread through that whole land. Soon he had nothing to eat.

He went to work for a man in that country, and the man sent him out to take care of his pigs. He would have been glad to eat what the pigs were eating, but no one gave him a thing.

Finally, he came to his senses and said, "My father's workers have plenty to eat, and here I am, starving to death! I will go to my father and say to him, 'Father, I have sinned against God in heaven and against you. I am no longer good enough to be called your son. Treat me like one of your workers.'"

The younger son got up and started back to his father. But when he was still a long way off, his father saw him and felt sorry for him. He ran to his son and hugged and kissed him.

The son said, "Father, I have sinned against God in heaven and against you. I am no longer good enough to be called your son."

But his father said to the servants, "Hurry and bring the best clothes and put them on him. Give him a ring for his finger and sandals for his feet. Get the best calf and prepare it, so we can eat and celebrate. This son of mine was dead, but has now come back to life. He was lost and has now been found." And they began to celebrate.

A country far away

Many Jews left Judea to try to make a living elsewhere. Some people estimate that there were about four million Jews scattered around the world.

The Pigs

The Law of Moses taught that pigs were unclean animals. Anyone who came into contact with pigs became ritually unclean and was not allowed to take part in the Sabbath prayers.

Kissed Him

The father's kiss is a sign of his forgiveness. It is followed by other signs, new clothes (a sign that he was rescued and restored to his family), new shoes (a sign of being a free person), and the best calf (a sign of a family feast).

The Prodigal Father

Better

Sometimes we accuse others of lying, of not keeping their promises, of behaving badly as Christians, and of many other things. Why? Maybe it's to keep ourselves from noticing the sin that we keep within us. Or perhaps it's so that we can say, "At least our hands are clean. We listen to God's word. What's more, we don't break the law. We don't use bad language or have bad thoughts!" So we think that we are better than others and that God should treat us better. Where does such pride come from?

Going far off

Sin is about turning away from God. When we sin, we turn our backs and go off. It's as if we say, "I can find better ways to be happy. With you, God, things are too strict and too difficult. I don't have space to organize my life the way I want. You get in the way of my doing what I want, so I'm getting away from you!"

Coming back

Conversion means turning back to God. It means turning our lives toward God. It's as if we would say, "It's a mistake to be away from you. We end up lost in the dark. With you, we find happiness. We find the light that shows us the way to go. Real happiness is being with you, accepting your love and your word that calls us to grow. You help us to be free!"

Open Arms

God's love is abundant. God pours out love on all people no matter who they are. No one has a better place with God than anyone else. Those who leave, those who stay, those who come back, saints and sinners… all are God's children and God loves them with the same love. God does not condemn those who wander off. God can hardly wait for them to come back, to welcome them with open arms. God is like a loving father, happy to find his lost children again!

Looking for Happiness

Lord, we try to get away,
set on having our own say,
like children blind to love at home
wanting to be left alone.

"Somewhere else I will be free!
God's way is much too hard for me.
The path of truth is steep and rough:
Forgiving once seems quite enough.
It's hard to share all that is mine.
It's hard to trust God all the time."

So, Lord, we try to get away
set on having our own say.
Pretending that we have not heard
the message of your gospel word.

But still its light calls us to you,
to happiness and love that's true,
to loving arms held open wide,
to someone always on our side.

How soon we miss the path
and stray
without your word
to light the way!

CHAPTER 5

The Parable of the Talents

Fra Giovanni da Fiesole, known as **Fra Angelico** (1400-1455), "The Last Judgment"

When this artist was painting, many people could not read. His pictures told stories to help people know the Gospel message. What is this picture saying about God? How does the artist express his message about good and evil?

© Scala, Saint Mark Museum, Florence (Italy)

What Jesus Said

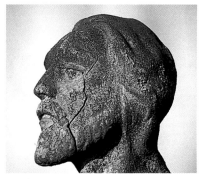
"Christ" (Luxembourg)

Jesus often talked about servants.* This word could mean slaves, but it also refers to a person who has been given an important responsibility. In the Bible, kings, prophets and judges were thought of as servants of God. When Jesus spoke about servants, he was thinking of the leaders of the people. It was their job to prepare people for the Kingdom of God. He was talking about the high priests, the scribes and the Pharisees.

Jesus taught that some religious leaders were bad servants. High priests were under Rome's thumb. Scribes explained the word of God poorly. Pharisees were concerned only about keeping every detail of the Law. Through the parable of the talents, Jesus tells them that the day will come when they will have to give an account of what they have done. Then the master will get rid of the bad servants.

"Treasure Trove" (Ireland)

In Matthew's Gospel

"Saint Matthew," the Church of St Peter in Gallicantu, Jerusalem

About fifty years after Jesus lived and taught in Galilee, Matthew wrote his Gospel, including the parable of the talents. Matthew was also thinking about the early Christians. Lots of things had changed. Jesus was no longer with them,** but they understood that Jesus was the "Lord," their true master and the master of God's servants. There were no high priests any more.*** The scribes had little or no influence among Christians. Jesus had given them a treasure that they must put to good use so that it would bear fruit. Some of the Christians had many talents, others a few. Some could do many things and were very dynamic, while others were less so. But it didn't really depend on them. What counted was to serve others by using the skills and talents they had received.

* Servants
Some of these servants are faithful, hardworking and wide awake. Others are unfaithful, lazy, and sleepy.

** Jesus was no longer with them
Matthew's Gospel was written in the 80's A.D. The parable of the talents is also contained in Luke's Gospel (19.11-27) where it is called the Parable of the Gold Coins.

*** No more high priests
After the Temple was destroyed in A.D. 70, the high priests, the priests who served at the Temple, and the Levites had no official jobs.

Good and Faithful Servant

Matthew 25.14-28

The kingdom is also like what happened when a man went away and put his three servants in charge of all he owned. The man knew what each servant could do. So he handed five thousand coins to the first servant, two thousand to the second, and one thousand to the third. Then he left the country.

As soon as the man had gone, the servant with the five thousand coins used them to earn five thousand more. The servant who had two thousand coins did the same with his money and earned two thousand more. But the servant with one thousand coins dug a hole and hid his master's money in the ground.

Some time later the master of those servants returned. He called them in and asked what they had done with his money. The servant who had been given five thousand coins brought them in with the five thousand that he had earned. He said, "Sir, you gave me five thousand coins, and I have earned five thousand more."

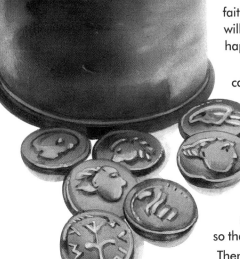

"Wonderful!" his master replied. "You are a good and faithful servant. I left you in charge of only a little, but now I will put you in charge of much more. Come and share in my happiness!"

Next, the servant who had been given two thousand coins came in and said, "Sir, you gave me two thousand coins, and I have earned two thousand more."

"Wonderful!" his master replied. "You are a good and faithful servant. I left you in charge of only a little, but now I will put you in charge of much more. Come and share in my happiness!"

The servant who had been given one thousand coins then came in and said, "Sir, I know that you are hard to get along with. You harvest what you don't plant and gather crops where you haven't scattered seed. I was frightened and went out and hid your money in the ground. Here is every single coin!"

The master of the servant told him, "You are lazy and good-for-nothing! You know that I harvest what I don't plant and gather crops where I haven't scattered seed. You could have at least put my money in the bank, so that I could have earned interest on it."

Then the master said, "Now your money will be taken away and given to the servant with ten thousand coins!"

Five Talents

A talent was large amount of money. It weighed over eighty pounds and was equivalent to about $1,000 in gold.

After a Long Time

The first Christians were waiting for the LORD to come back. But they did not know on what day or at what hour it would be, and it was taking a long time for him to return. For them, when the LORD left them, it was like a man going on a journey and giving his servants the job of making his business flourish while they waited for him to come back.

Share My Happiness

This refers to happiness in heaven, which is sometimes in the Scriptures referred to as a big banquet. The unfaithful servants, however, are not allowed to attend.

The Treasure Is within You

Enabled

Each one of us has a treasure we can truly call our very own. It is our own self and all that makes us who we are. Out of this treasure comes our power to think deeply and individually. We can "enter into" our own mind and heart and quietly allow our inner self to examine questions and imagine possible answers. This power is God's gift. Out of it comes the marvelous variety of all our other gifts. Out of it comes our energy for life. It's what makes us tick! It is the gift of God in whose image each of us is created.

Waste

What's the point of this treasure if we don't stir ourselves to action? What's the point of these amazing riches if we don't use them? What a waste they would be! It's as if we said to God, "I'm not interested in these gifts. I want something else." The power to love, to create, to plan for the future, to live and work in unity, to believe – just think what would happen if everyone were to let these gifts lie dormant and unused? Can we let them remain buried instead of using them to create and do things? What a waste!

Developing

If we're going to respond to the trust God has placed in us, we have to develop our skills. We have to work on them just as people work on a garden to make it produce beautiful fruit and flowers. What a responsibility! We can use our gifts and abilities to co-operate with God in creating things. Or we can let the gifts God has given us go to waste!

A Work of Art

By using our gifts each of us can make our life into a wonderful work of art for ourselves and for others. That's what God asks us to do. This story is about letting our talents blossom and using them to serve others. This is the "service" that God wants from us. Faithful servants use their gifts and work with God to create a world where everyone feels loved and people live as brothers and sisters, a world made in the image and likeness of God.

Enabled

I have the power to see and love
the light that shines in another's face;
to see the goodness and beauty within
when on the surface there's not a trace.

I have the power to let myself
be caught up in praise by the dancing light
of a sunset sky dressed in red and gold
as evening deepens into night.

I have the power to dance with joy
on a carpet of music rolled out for me
when the notes fill my ears and spill
into my heart so powerfully.

I have the power to laugh and cry,
to be comforted and comfort give,
to choose evil or good and make the world
a worse or better place to live.

I have the power to give and receive
love and friendship again and again.
I have the power to forgive, to rejoice
and to praise God's holy name.

Here I am, Lord, here, I come
with all the gifts you have given me:
to love my neighbor and each day
to serve you faithfully.

Life at the Time of Jesus

The gospels contain thirty-nine parables of Jesus. To understand them fully, we have to look for a deeper meaning. That's what we have done with the five parables in this book. But we can also read the parables in another way. We can look at them and learn about the country of Jesus and what life was like in his day. In fact, Jesus told these stories using things he saw around him. We don't have any photographs from that period. But the parables teach us a lot of things about nature and about how people lived in Jesus' day.

Nature

Seeds are sown. They sprout up by themselves and they produce many different fruits. The little mustard seed turns into a great tree. The fig tree flowers and lets us know that summer is here. Weeds sometimes choke crops. Pretty lilies cover the meadows. Birds flock together in the sky and go in search of food.

Storks (Syria)

Work

The sower goes out to sow. The shepherd goes in search of the lost sheep. The fisherman casts his net. The owner of a vineyard takes on workmen and pays them. Other workers in a vineyard rebel against their employer. The doorman falls asleep while waiting for his master to come back. Some builders construct a tower. A king goes off to battle.

A fisherman, Nha Tvang (Vietnam)

Money

Some people are rich and others, like Lazarus, are poor. Many people have to go into debt. Officials, sometimes honest and sometimes dishonest, manage the money affairs of their employers. Some rich people are so consumed with their money that they forget they will die one day. A housewife looks for some money she has lost. Occasionally a surprise lies in store and people find a pearl or a piece of treasure hidden in a field.

Family

A mother prepares bread with leaven. A lamp is placed on a shelf to give light to the house. Children play in the square. Sons are both obedient and rebellious. Some leave home. Feasts are important, especially weddings. Bridesmaids accompany the groom. You have to be well dressed to get in. You shouldn't choose the best place at the table.

Jerusalem Market

Society

Judges are sometimes unjust. You have to keep asking them for justice. Samaritans are looked down on. The priests and Levites are not as helpful as you might think. Tax collectors are despised and Pharisees show off. It's good to have a friend you can ask for a favor.

So, while the parables were written to teach about the Kingdom of God, they also teach us what life was like in the days of Jesus.

Titles already published:

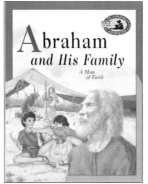
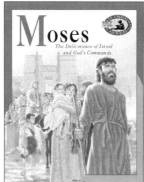
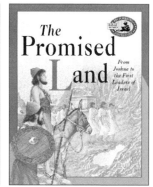

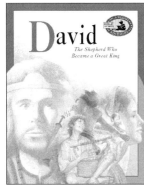

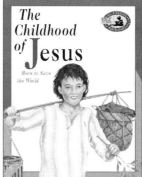
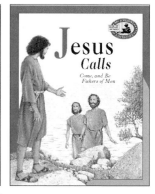

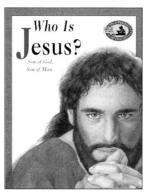
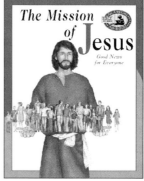

Forthcoming titles in the JUNIOR BIBLE Collection:

- The First Prophets
- Passion and Resurrection
- Exile and Return
- Isaiah, Micah, Jeremiah
- Jesus and the Outcasts
- Jesus in Jerusalem
- Acts
- Wisdom
- Psalms
- Women
- Revelation
- Letters

The Land of Jesus

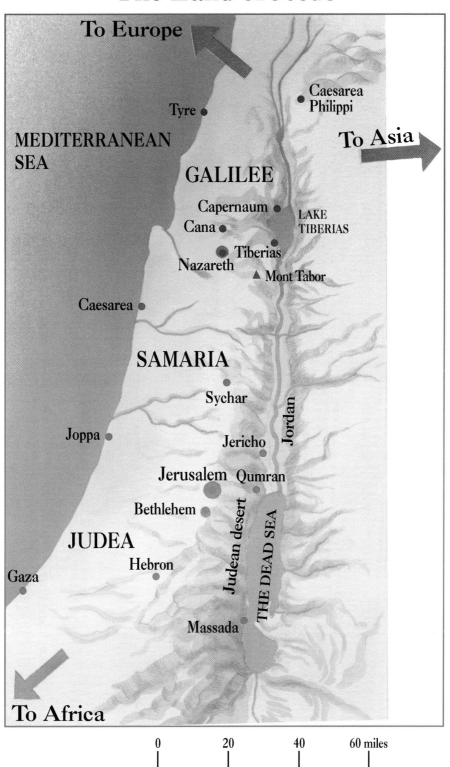

To Europe

To Asia

MEDITERRANEAN
SEA

Tyre

Caesarea
Philippi

GALILEE

Capernaum

Cana

LAKE
TIBERIAS

Tiberias

Nazareth

▲ Mont Tabor

Caesarea

SAMARIA

Sychar

Jordan

Joppa

Jericho

Jerusalem   Qumran

Bethlehem

Judean desert

THE DEAD SEA

JUDEA

Hebron

Gaza

Massada

To Africa

| 0 | 20 | 40 | 60 miles |

The Parables of Jesus

ORIGINAL TEXT BY

Liam KELLY, Anne WHITE,

Albert HARI, Charles SINGER

ENGLISH TEXT ADAPTED BY

the American Bible Society

PHOTOGRAPHY

Frantisek ZVARDON

ILLUSTRATORS

Mariano VALSESIA, Betti FERRERO

MIA. Milan Illustrations Agency

LAYOUT

Bayle Graphic Studio

FIRST PRINTING: NOVEMBER 2000

For information write: Master Books, P.O. Box 727, Green Forest, AR 72638.

ISBN: 0-89051-331-7

ÉDITIONS
DU SIGNE
© ÉDITIONS DU SIGNE 1997